The little book of good behaviour

Text and illustrations by Christine Coirault

for more books visit
www.frogillo.com/books

First published by Frogillo Books, 2005
copyright Frogillo Books 2005

ISBN
0954854810

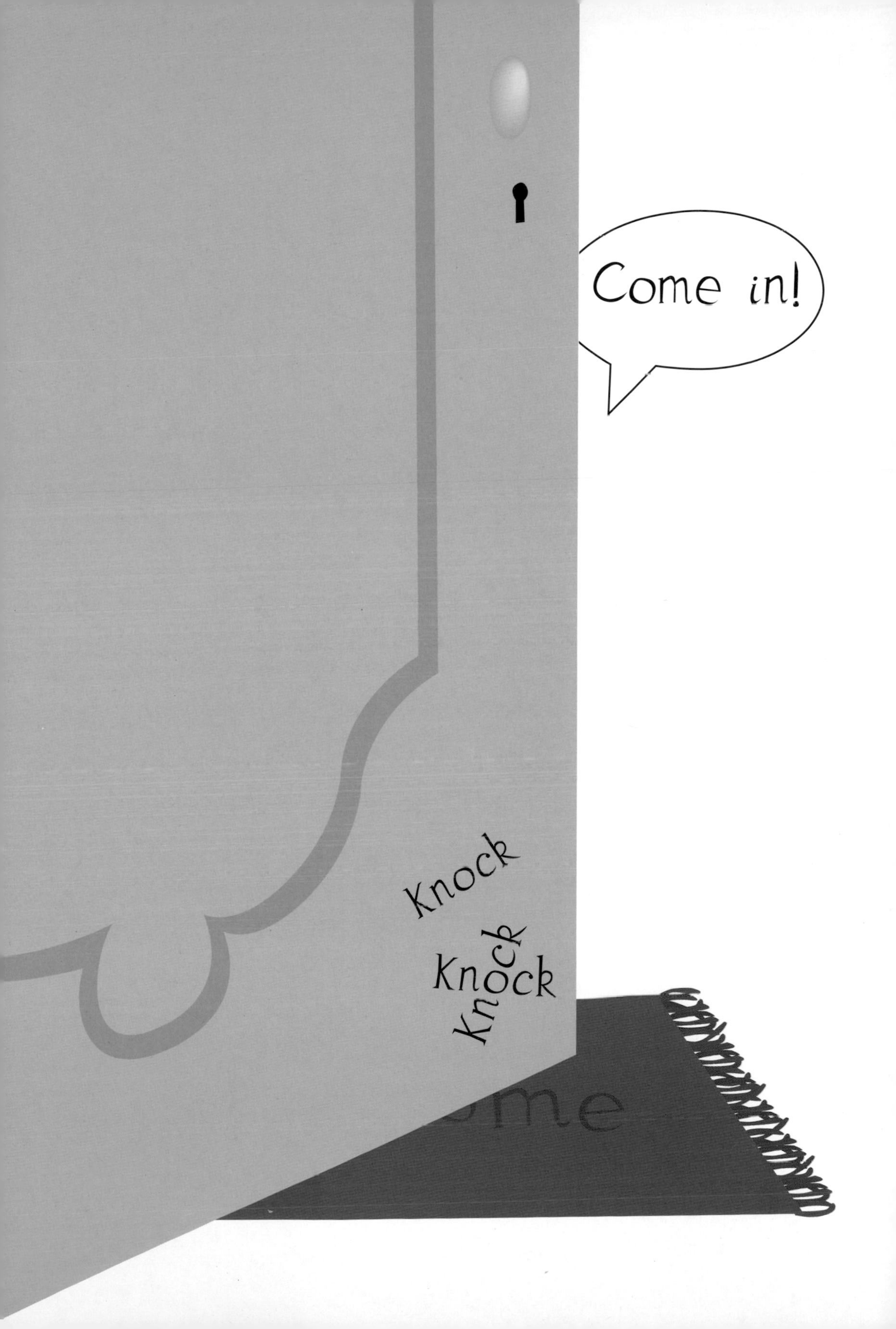
Come in!
Knock
Knock
Knock

Before
going in
Millie wipes
every
single one
of her feet.

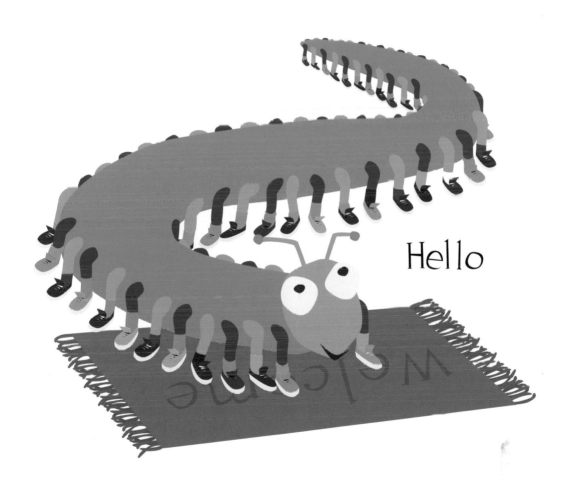

Hello

Whenever someone needs a hand...

...Lola is
always
the first
to help.

When Robbie
meets a friend,
he makes sure he
gets there on time.

If he needs to change
his plans, he lets
his friend know
as soon as possible.

Crossing
the road
can be tricky
for anyone...

...fortunately, Lolly helps

everybody to cross safely.

Splash!
Splash!

Splash!
Splash!

Mind your steps Tammy, Douggie needs to keep dry for school!

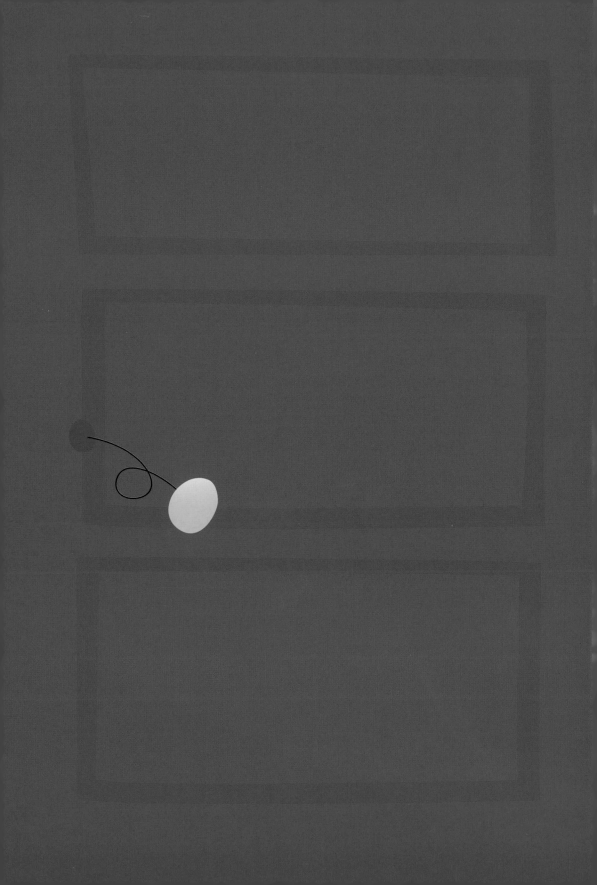

...it's a nuisance.

Respect
others'
peace
and quiet
at home...

...and in public

places, too!

Gum is fun
to chew
and to blow
bubbles with...

...but what a
sticky mess it makes
on the ground!

Kim keeps wrappers in her pouch until she finds a rubbish bin.

Monica washes
her hands
before
every meal.

A cake is
for sharing.
Even if it means
giving the
biggest
slice away!

Keeping clean
is never a
problem for
Stanley, as
he always uses
a knife and fork.

After every meal,

Ali brushes his
teeth thoroughly.

Goodbye for now!